THE CONCISE
Kama Sutra

ANNE JOHNSON

Based on the original translation by
SIR RICHARD BURTON

hamlyn

First published in Great Britain in 2000 by

Hamlyn, a division of Octopus Publishing Group Limited,

2-4 Heron Quays, Docklands, London, E14 4JP

Copyright © 2000 Octopus Publishing Group

ISBN 0 600 59938 8

A CIP catalogue record of this book is available from the
British Library

Printed in China

THE CONCISE
Kama Sutra

ANNE JOHNSON

Based on the original translation by

SIR RICHARD BURTON

hamlyn

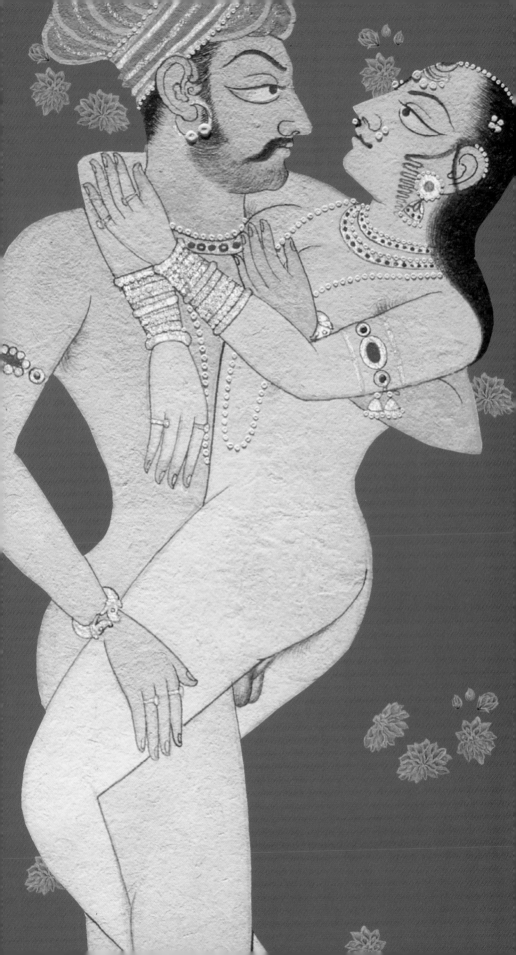

~ contents ~

Introduction

The *Kama Sutra* is one of the oldest and most famous works of eroticism ever written. It is also one of the most readable and the most enjoyable.

Unfortunately, however, and still in the more liberated times of today, the *Kama Sutra* is generally regarded as a sex manual or, worst still, as a pillow book, or even as pornography. Yet nothing could be less pornographic, and nor should it be treated as a step-by-step love manual. It is refreshingly candid, it is undeniably frank, and it is at times outspoken, but it is by no means dirty. And in spite its reputation, it does not even deal exclusively with sex. There's a lot more to it than that and it also deals with the much broader issues of society, culture, politics, economy, philosophy and morality.

Its main aim is as a treatise on the art of living (of which sex is but one aspect) for the well-bred and civilized citizen.

It is, in fact, a meticulously written guide to sexual and social etiquette for the leisured classes of ancient India. The title means 'the science of pleasure' and the tone of the book is almost clinical, even academic, which sometimes presents an unintentionally amusing contrast with the subject matter.

But sex is what we're talking about here, and it is probably true to say that there is no better way of understanding people than to enter into their sexual lives. Sex is a good way to begin to understand another culture, just as it is a good way of beginning to understand another individual.

Vatsyayana

The author of the *Kama Sutra* was a man called Mallinaga
Vatsyayana, about whom very little is known. He was a
Brahman and a man of letters, who lived in the city of
Pataliputra some time around the fourth century AD.

He was, in fact, as much the compiler of the work as the
author, and he did not claim his work to be an original one.
He does state, however, that he had himself verified all the
practices that he describes in it through personal experience.

His sources included the vast body of Hindu erotology,
which already existed by the first century AD. By the time
Vatsyayana came to compile his work, many of his sources
had already become difficult for people to get hold of, with
the result that he determined to collect and summarize them
in his *Kama Sutra*. It was this that was to become the classic
work on the subject, which is undeniably stamped with the
personality of the old sage.

A 'sutra' is an aphorism, written in a condensed and versified
form, which makes the briefest possible statement of a
principle. The idea was that it was intended to be memorized
with explanations provided by a teacher. The sutra was
probably favoured in all Hindu technical works, because
writing was not widespread during this period and students
could memorize important texts more easily. All the
important Sanskrit works on logic, grammar and philosophy
were written in sutras, including the dictionary, as well as
grammar and scientific treatises.

Thus the commentaries are an integral part of the teaching. Vatsyayana speaks of himself modestly in the third person when he adds an opinion of his own: 'Vatsyayana's opinion is that . . .' and so on.

Worldly-wise but not world-weary, Vatsyayana approaches his subject with an impartiality and a detachment that are sometimes almost clinical. Yet it is a human book above all else, a masterpiece of tolerance and good sense. Although 'some learned men object', Vatsyayana insists that women should read his work; he argues the case with his usual blend of pragmatism and humanity.

It should not be forgotten that Vatsyayana compiled this book many centuries ago. In spite of that, it is surprising that it still retains a remarkable topicality and relevance to our lives today. It is a book of love which is valid for all times and places in the world.

All the later Indian writers could only follow the old sage, and indeed through the centuries the least among them acknowledge the fact. In the *Kama Sutra*, Vatsyayana wrote one of the great books of the world, capturing a world of enchantment, pleasure and sensation.

Translation

The first translation of the *Kama Sutra* was produced by Sir Richard Burton, who was a well-known nineteenth-century explorer, anthropologist and linguist. His translation first appeared in 1883 when it shocked an unsuspecting world. Its republication in the liberated 1960s was regarded then as one of the important literary events of the century.

His translations included several erotic works other than the *Kama Sutra*, such as the *Arabian Nights* and *The Perfumed Garden*, and he was frequently at risk of prosecution under the Obscene Publications Act of 1857. Burton spoke 25 languages and many dialects, and travelled the world extensively.

Burton's is not the only translation of the *Kama Sutra*, but it is the oldest and probably the most widely quoted. An excellent modern translation was done recently in the early 1990s by Alain Daniélou, a leading Orientalist and an expert on Hindu religion, society, music and art, which has gained the respect of many scholars.

a life
of
pleasure

Having first acquired the
necessary learning in his
childhood, a man ~ using the
riches that he may have gained
either by gift, conquest, purchase
or inheritance ~ should then
become a responsible householder
and spend the life of a wealthy
citizen. This is a life of luxury,
easy pleasure and entertainment.

A harmonious life

During the three principal periods of a man's life ~ these
being childhood, middle age and old age ~ he must pursue
the three principal aims of life in turn. In other words, a man
must realize himself on three different levels, all of which are
interdependent and present throughout all ages of his life.
Childhood, which is the period up until the age of about
sixteen, must be dedicated to the acquisition of knowledge,
including the all-important skills of reading and counting as
well as the sciences, which he must learn with respected
masters and scholars. At this time he must remain chaste.
Then, in adulthood, he must practise both Artha ~ which is
the acquisition of arts and material wealth, including land,
gold, cattle, furniture, friends and clothing ~ and Kama,
which is the practice of love, eroticism and the consciousness
of the pleasures of the five senses, including hearing, touch,
sight, taste and smell, all of which are learned with the help
of the *Kama Sutra*. And then finally, in old age, he must
dedicate himself to Dharma, which is the practice of virtue,
spiritualism, ritual sacrifice and such conduct as is required
by the teachings of the scriptures.

*Man, the period of whose life is one hundred years, should
practise Dharma, Artha and Kama at different times and in such a
manner that they may harmonize. He should together acquire learning
in his childhood, in his youth and middle age he should attend to
Artha and Kama, and in his old age he should perform Dharma.*

Kama Sutra

Man's three principal aims

Kama is to be learned from a concentrated study of the *Kama Sutra* and from the practice of fellow citizens ~ but eroticism, while it is essential for the survival of man, just as food is also necessary for his very existence, is not the only factor that deserves to be taken seriously in life. It is only one of man's three principal aims. And it is the man who looks after all three of his aims of life, including all matters of wealth, love and virtue, and who deliberately chooses those ways of behaviour that allow him to achieve all three, who is most likely to succeed, effortlessly and painlessly, in his overall aim of attaining the maximum possible state of bliss both in this world and in the next. Allowing the exaggerated pursuit of any one of these aims ~ be it a question of riches, duty or pleasure ~ to dominate everything else in life is likely to interfere with the attainment of any of the others. Conversely, failure in any single one of his three principal aims can hinder the achievement of all of them, which will stand in the way of his attainment of happiness.

This work is not intended to be used merely as an instrument for satisfying our desires. A person . . . who preserves his Dharma, Artha, and Kama, and has regard for the practices of the people, is most likely to obtain the mastery over his senses . . . and to obtain success in everything that he may undertake.

Kama Sutra

The lover's home

The ideal citizen is a householder and takes an abode in a
city, or a large village, where there are other persons of good
society. The house should be situated near some water and is
surrounded by a garden with one whirling swing and
another simple swing, as well as a bower of beautiful creepers
covered in flowers with a raised parterre below it made for
sitting. The house has two rooms ~ an outer one and an
inner one. The inner room is occupied by the women,
while the outer one is a bedroom, where the air is heady
with rich perfumes. The bed is covered in a clean white
cloth and has garlands and bunches of flowers placed upon
it. There are songbirds in cages and, on a nearby couch, there
are pots with fragrant ointments for the night. Near the
couch, there is a pot for spitting, a box containing
ornaments, a lute hanging from a peg made from an
elephant's tooth, a board for playing with dice, books,
drawing materials and separate places for spinning, carving,
and other similar diversions. There should also be some
garlands of the yellow amaranth flowers.

*The outer room . . . should contain a bed, soft, agreeable to the
sight . . . and two pillows, one at the top, another at the bottom. There
should be . . . placed the fragrant ointments for the night, as well as
flowers, pots containing collyrium and other fragrant substances,
things used for the mouth, and the bark of the common citron tree.*

Kama Sutra

The lover's day

On rising early in the morning, the well-bred townsman performs a careful and elaborate toilet. This includes washing his teeth with a special preparation of scented ingredients, applying various unguents and fragrances to his body, and carefully making up his eyes and mouth. He should then eat betel leaves to give a pleasant fragrance to his mouth. He should also bathe every day ~ particularly before taking food ~ anoint his body with oil and have a massage every other day, and soap himself every three days to soften his skin. Every four days, he must trim his beard and his moustache into three points, and on the fifth or tenth day he must also have a barber shave his body hair, including his armpits and his pubic hair, leaving the area free for sexual activity. All of these things must be done without fail, and the sweat of the armpits should always be meticulously removed. He should always perfume himself assiduously to mask the unpleasant smell of sweat from the armpits and to make him pleasant to be close to.

How the householder, having got up in the morning and performed his necessary duties, should wash his teeth, apply a limited quantity of ointments and perfumes to his body, put some ornaments on his person and collyrium on his eyelids and below his eyes, colour his lips with alacktaka, and look at himself in the glass. Having then eaten betel leaves . . . he should perform his usual business.

Kama Sutra

The lover's way of life

Meals are taken in the morning after bathing, and then only a small quantity of food in the afternoon and again in the evening, though the digestion should be complete before eating again. Food eaten by the ancient Hindus was of four kinds ~ that which was chewed, that which was licked, that which was sucked and that which was drunk. Common foods included wheat, rice, rye, chickpeas, lentils, ghee (clarified butter) and meat. Salt biscuits preceded the main dishes and sweet dishes finished the meal. After meals, quiet amusements were in order, such as teaching mynah birds and parrots to talk, both of which were popular companions, with whom people formed close relationships. Birds were also used to carry messages between lovers and ~ in time of war ~ secret messages and instructions. Men also enjoyed watching fights between cocks, partridges and rams. Teaching birds to talk and watching animal fights all belonged to the sixty-four doctrines of pleasure for an accomplished suitor. Some time might also be spent meeting with one's manager, comrade or secretary, all of whom fulfilled the role of go-between for the man-about-town of the time ~ talking about his appointments and disputes. A siesta was customary after this and was believed to rest and strengthen the body.

Meals should be taken in the forenoon, in the afternoon and again at night, according to Charayana. After breakfast, parrots and other birds should be taught to speak, and the fighting of cocks, quails, and rams should follow . . . After this the householder, having put on his clothes and ornaments, should, during the afternoon, converse with his friends.

Kama Sutra

The lover's pastimes

The citizen would then dress himself elegantly, with fine silk and wool clothes and precious jewels such as diamonds, pears, emeralds and rubies. He would also bedeck himself with beautiful garlands of fresh and colourful flowers in preparation for his attendance at a grand reception. Many people, such as musicians, actors, singers and dancers, were often known to congregate in the evening for this purpose, to which many distinguished and cultured guests were invited, such as scholars, poets and specialists in ancient history or legendary epics. The evening entertainment might be a concert, a play, a ballad, or the telling of poetry and heroic tales, with much singing and dancing. After the evening reception, the well-bred townsman would then go back to his abode, where his preferred lady friend would be waiting for him in his bedroom, or perhaps he might send a female messenger to fetch her, or he might go and fetch her himself. After her arrival at his house, he and his friend would welcome her and entertain her with conversation, which would be both loving and pleasant. This brought the activities of the day to a happy and agreeable conclusion.

In the evening there should be singing, and after that the householder, along with his friend, should await in his room, previously decorated and perfumed, the arrival of the woman that may be attached to him, or he may send a female messenger for her, or go to her himself . . . Thus end the duties of the day.

Kama Sutra

Diversions and amusements

There were many kinds of diversion that would be organized
to entertain the citizen, such as seasonal festivities, picnics
and social gatherings, most of which took place in the
gardens or in someone's home. Some gatherings took place
to discuss matters of art and literature, while others took
place at special feasts and at the sanctuary of various
goddesses, such as Sarasvati, who was patron of dancing and
music. Strangers had to be welcomed respectfully to all these
festivals, even if they were not among the invited guests.
There were also drinking parties, which took place at a fixed
and regular date each fortnight or month, at which guests
drank wine, strong liquor such as rum, which was made from
molasses or mango juice and spices, and mead. Intoxicating
drinks were thought to give strength and courage, as well as
stimulating the eroticism of the gentlemen, and courtesans
were often also present for this purpose. Guests ate salty
appetizers, fiery sweetmeats, spicy dishes and salads. Bracing
country walks, during which the citizen gathered fruits and
flowers, and pleasure rides on horseback were also popular
and were thought to be especially good for the health. Fine
weather necessitated water games, which took place at a
reservoir or pond, free from crocodiles.

*The following are the things to be done occasionally as diversions
or amusements: holding festivals in honour of different Deities, social
gatherings of both sexes, drinking parties, picnics and other social
diversions.*

Kama Sutra

the Kama Shastras

For sexual intercourse to be a happy and successful experience, it is essential to develop a sound knowledge of erotic technique. At the core of this, there are sixty-four doctrines of pleasure, which every accomplished suitor needs to have at his disposal both for his own pleasure and for that of his consorts.

Erotic technique

A sound knowledge of erotic technique is essential to happy and successful sexual intercourse. The penis should not be introduced into the woman without extensive preliminary loveplay, and there are sixty-four elements involved in this. As a body of techniques, these are known collectively as 'sixty-four'. Several explanations have been put forward to explain this choice of name. It may be, quite simply, because they were originally outlined in sixty-four chapters. It may be, on the other hand, because the author of this particular section was someone called Panchala, and the great sage who recited the part of the *Rig Veda* that was divided into sixty-four verses was also called Panchala; it is thus out of respect for these erotic learnings that they are compared, by use of this name, with the great sacred text. The followers of Babhravya offer yet another, even simpler explanation for the choice of name: these people say that there are known to be eight categories of erotic practice, each of which is, in turn, made up of eight different kinds ~ and eight times eight is, of course, sixty-four.

This part of the Kama Shastra, which treats of sexual union, is also called 'Sixty-four' . . . The followers of Babhravya say . . . that this part contains eight subjects: the embrace, kissing, scratching with the nails or fingers, biting, lying down, making various sounds, playing the part of a man, and the Auparishtaka, or mouth congress. Each of these subjects being of eight kinds, and eight multiplied by eight being sixty-four, this part is . . . named 'Sixty-four'.

Kama Sutra

Sexual characteristics

A man is strong and dominant, while a woman is timid and weak. These are the natural characteristics displayed by the two sexes. Their different and often opposing temperaments play a large part in their relations ~ he aggressive and domineering, she frail and acquiescent. It is this that leads a man to attack a woman and a woman, in turn, to put up with it and to groan in response. At its extreme, the result of this is that the passionate man may actually enjoy beating a woman, even if this means that he has to inflict pain on her, while a woman often enjoys receiving those blows and actively wants to be beaten ~ something that she indicates to him by a series of sighs and groans. Sometimes the woman may put aside her natural tendencies and she may encourage a reversal of roles. Gender characteristics are not always universal, and a woman is only likely to become sufficiently hard and determined and to lose her fear in certain countries or under certain circumstances, so this role reversal does not happen very often. Even when it does occur, it does not usually last for long, and the roles will soon revert to normality.

The characteristics of manhood are said to consist of roughness and impetuosity, while weakness, tenderness, sensibility, and an inclination to turn away from unpleasant things are the distinguishing marks of womanhood. The excitement of passion, and peculiarities of habit, may sometimes cause contrary results to appear, but these do not last long . . .

Kama Sutra

When passion takes over

Kissing is an important part of lovemaking ~ as important, indeed, as any of the other things that two people can do to each other as part of their preliminary loveplay, such as scratching, slapping and biting, all of which help to cause the arousal that is necessary prior to intercourse. According to Vatsyayana, when a couple is seized by passion, there is no particular order in which they should perform any of these things ~ love takes no notice of time or order, rhyme or reason, in these matters. There are no rules. To start with, it is important not to spend too long concentrating on any one thing. Everything should be done gently, carefully, slowly and in moderation, until sufficient confidence has been reached to progress further. It is not, in any case, possible to do everything at once, so each thing should be done in turn. The order in which you should do these things is dictated by both desire and confidence, which should increase simultaneously. As this happens, self-control and the need for moderation cease to be such important factors and a lasting relationship between desire and intercourse should become possible.

Vatsyayana . . . thinks that anything may take place at any time, for love does not care for time or order. On the occasion of the first congress, kissing and the other things mentioned above should be done moderately, they should not be continued for a long time, and should be done alternately.

Kama Sutra

Size matters

While taking into account matters of personal preference, there are different methods of penetration which are best suited to particular couples, depending on their size and the size of their sexual organs. The deer woman, for example, or the woman with a small vagina, or yoni, who is in partnership with a horse man, or a man with a large penis, should take care to lie down in such a way as to open her vagina as wide as possible. There are three ways in which she can do this: she can lower her head and raise her central body, which is called the widely opened position; or she can raise her thighs and keep them wide apart, which is called the yawning position; or she can bend her thighs back against each other, which is called the position of Indrani and is learned only by practice. An elephant woman, on the other hand, or a woman with a large vagina, who is in a relationship with a hare man, or a man with a small penis, should lie down in such a way as to contract her sex. When the man and woman are of well-matched sizes, the woman need neither stretch nor contract her organ.

On the occasion of a 'high congress' the Mirigi (deer) woman should lie down in such a way as to widen her yoni, while in a 'low congress' the Hastini (elephant) woman should lie down so as to contract hers. But in an 'equal congress' they should lie in the natural position.

Kama Sutra

Man's work

Whatever is done in order to give pleasure to a woman is regarded as the work of a man. This is done as follows: while she is lying on his bed and he is distracting her attention with his tender words, he should pay attention to loosening her underwear. If she tries to protest, he should embrace her passionately and overwhelm her with his kisses. Then, when his penis has become erect, he should cover her body with his hands and touch her all over, gently and slowly. If she is shy and if this is the first time that they have been together in this way, he should place his hands between her thighs, which she may attempt to keep closed together. He should also put his hands on her breasts, which she may try to cover with her own hands. He should take hold of her hair and hold her chin in his hands while he kisses her. A young girl may be bashful and close her eyes, but he should be able to tell what things are pleasing to her, especially if she is an adult woman of some experience.

While the woman is lying on his bed, . . . he should loosen the knot of her undergarments, and when she begins to dispute with him, he should overwhelm her with kisses. Then when his lingam is erect, he should touch her with his hands in various places, and gently manipulate various parts of her body.

Kama Sutra

The attentive lover

A man will concentrate on doing those things that he most
enjoys during lovemaking, but the attentive lover will always
make a point of attending to her needs and wants as well as
his own. The signs that a woman is enjoying the things that
are being done to her and that she is getting satisfaction from
her lovemaking should be obvious to her lover. Her body
will relax, she may close her eyes, and she will probably be
keen on bringing their two sexual organs ~ his and hers ~ as
close together as possible. If, on the other hand, she is not
enjoying his attentions and is not reaching satisfaction, that
should be obvious, too. She will probably shake her hands,
she will feel dejected, and she may even bite and kick the
man to show her annoyance. She will probably continue
moving after the man has come, showing that just because he
has reached a climax, he must not assume that she has, too. If
this is the case, the man should concentrate on stroking the
woman's vagina with his fingers until she is ready for him
and then, when she is satisfied, they should have full
penetrative sex.

*In such cases, the man should rub the yoni of the woman with
his hand and fingers (as the elephant rubs anything with his trunk)
before engaging in congress, until it is softened, and after that is done
he should proceed to put his lingam into her.*

Kama Sutra

~ *the kama shastras* ~

A respect for the doctrines

The accomplished suitor, who uses the sixty-four doctrines of Kama mentioned by Babhravya, will always enjoy the best women. Even though he may speak authoritatively on all sorts of other subjects, he will receive no respect in the company of learned men if he is not acquainted with the sixty-four erotic arts. An uneducated man who has no knowledge, on the other hand, but who is well versed in the sixty-four arts of erotic technique, will rapidly become the leader of any society, whether of men or women. Who could fail to develop a tremendous respect for the sixty-four doctrines, when they are held in such high esteem by so many people, from the most learned scholar to the simplest courtesan? His love life will soon become one of the highest quality. But this work is not intended to be used merely as an instrument for satisfying his physical desires. It is much more than that. The sixty-four arts are of the utmost importance and are sure to add to the erotic talent of all the women in his life ~ including his own dear wife, the wives of others, and courtesans of his acquaintance.

What man will not respect the sixty-four arts, considering they are respected by the learned, by the cunning, and by the courtesans . . . A man skilled in the sixty-four arts is looked upon with love by his own wife, by the wives of others, and by courtesans.

Kama Sutra

courtship

Albeit that polygamy was the normal practice in India during the fourth century AD, marriage was nonetheless a significant institution and was much sought after. The way in which a man chose and courted his bride was therefore considered to be of the utmost importance.

Of marriageable age

When a virgin of the same caste is married in accordance with the precepts of Holy Writ, the results of such a union are many. They include the acquisition of Dharma (virtue), Artha (wealth) and Kama (love), the birth of children, and a widening of one's social circle. A man should therefore fix his affections on a respectable, wealthy, well-connected girl of good family, who is at least three years younger than him, and whose parents are still alive. In order to bring about such a union, the parents of a girl who has attained a suitable age at which to be married should make every effort to arrange a meeting. They should dress her in beautiful clothes, bearing in mind that an object that is not attractively and luxuriously decorated is not likely to attract any buyers. They must make sure that she goes to all the right places in the evening with her friends, where she will be sure to be seen by as many people as possible. Her female companions should accompany her to the greatest possible number of social occasions, such as sporting fixtures, religious sacrifices and weddings, where she is likely to meet other people of a similar background and age group.

When a girl becomes marriageable her parents should dress her smartly, and should place her where she can be easily seen by all. Every afternoon, having dressed her and decorated her in a becoming manner, they should send her with her female companions to sports, sacrifices and marriage ceremonies, and thus show her to advantage in society.

Kama Sutra

The parents' role

The loving parents of the single girl who are keeping a careful eye on her future welfare should welcome all visitors to their house, with pleasant words and outward evidence of warmth and friendliness. This applies, in particular, to any potential suitors, who have come suitably dressed for the occasion and have first performed all the ceremonies that bring good luck before their visit. They will be accompanied by their friends and relatives for the express purpose of marrying their daughter. If the girl is asleep, or upset, or if she has gone out, or if she is already betrothed to someone else, she is not in a position to be married. Some people say that prosperity is acquired only by marrying the girl to whom one becomes attached and with whom one falls in love. Then, after making sure that she is smartly dressed and looking as attractive as possible ~ because she is rather like a piece of merchandise that needs to be viewed in a good light by potential buyers ~ the girl's parents should use some pretext or other to introduce them to one another. But he should only get a glimpse of her at this stage, with an indication of her luxurious ornaments and jewels ~ he should not see her properly until the moment of the handing over.

They should also receive with kind words and signs of friendliness those of an auspicious appearance who may come accompanied by their friends and relations for the purpose of marrying their daughter, and under some pretext or other, having first dressed her becomingly, should then present her to them.

Kama Sutra

Observing rituals

After this initial approach, they should then wait and see what happens and what fortune has in store for them. With this in mind, they should not agree with any request straight away but should rather settle on future dates ~ first for their next meeting at which they can come to an agreement about their daughter's marriage, and then for the marriage ceremony itself, in accordance with the omens which have been examined with the aid of her friends and family. The girl's parents should ask the suitor and his friends to take a ritual bath and to dine with them, and should tell them that 'everything will take place at the proper time' and they will not comply immediately but will settle the details later. The suitor, dressed in white, and his friends should then go to the altar of the funereal deities in order to pay his debt to his ancestors by making the four offerings to the dead. The ceremony will take place later, according to local tradition, when the man will marry her in accordance with the precepts of the holy scriptures. The priestly rite gives the daughter to her suitor, for both of them to 'together practise virtue'.

After this they should await the pleasure of fortune, and with this object should appoint a future day on which a determination could be come to with regard to their daughter's marriage. On this occasion, when the persons have come, the parents of the girl should . . . say, "Everything will take place at the proper time . . ."

Kama Sutra

The marriage of equals

It is important, if a happy marriage is to be successful, to understand that, although there are twenty-three forms of marriage, there are only four forms worthy of our consideration ~ these are priestly, royal, ancestral and astral. The priestly rite consists of saying, 'With a joyful heart I give you my daughter, covered with jewels.' The royal rite is a matter of pronouncing the formula, 'May you together practise virtue.' The ancestral rite is performed in exchange for the gift of two bulls. And the astral rite consists of taking a marriage vow at the domestic altar. It is only these four forms of marriage which conform to the prescription of the holy books. It is agreed, too, in the pursuit of a happy marriage, that one should associate with and marry one's equals ~ in other words, people who are part of one's own social circle and who are therefore neither superior nor inferior. Similarly, it is also best to work with people who are one's equals. The best relationships are also with people who follow the same religion and who therefore have the same system of values and follow the same principles. This leads to a state of harmony and happiness, whereas if two people have dramatically different value systems, they will find it much more difficult to succeed in having a good relationship.

Amusement in society, such as completing verses begun by others, marriage, and auspicious ceremonies should be carried on neither with superiors, nor inferiors, but with our equals.

Kama Sutra

An equal connection

A prudent man would be wise to avoid marrying a woman who is of vastly superior status, as this would mean, after their marriage, that he would end up leading the life of a servant ~ constantly in obeisance to his wife's whims and desires and those of her equally superior relations. This is known as 'a high connection' and is particularly likely to happen if she is rich and he is poor, which would underline the inequality of their relationship. Similarly, the man who marries a woman who is vastly inferior to himself is likely to behave as a master and the woman as his slave. A prudent man will avoid this kind of marriage, which does not stand much chance of being a happy one. This is known as 'a low connection' and is particularly likely to happen if she is poor and he is rich, which again underlines the inequality of their relationship. Broadly speaking, such unequal relationships are not advised, in as much as the way of life of the two people involved is so different and so, correspondingly, are their relations with other people. A couple is much more likely to establish a good relationship if they are equals and their relationship starts on the same footing.

That should be known as a high connection when a man, after marrying a girl, has to serve her and her relations afterwards like a servant, and such a connection is censured by the good. On the other hand, that reproachable connection, where a man lords it over his wife, is called a low connection by the wise.

Kama Sutra

Sharing the same values

When, on the other hand, two people come from the same background and are therefore of much the same status and thus similarly rich or poor, they have a much better chance of establishing a happy and lasting relationship. But an equal relationship means a lot more than simply having the same amount of money. It also means having the same interests, the same tastes, the same outlook, the same expectations, the same ambitions, the same ideals, and the same values. Such a couple are extremely lucky and stand a high chance of success in the marriage stakes. They are likely to find that they are virtually always in basic agreement with one another. This, in turn, is likely to reinforce and thus to enhance each other's values, and this will probably do a great deal to strengthen their relationship. Such an equal relationship is therefore strongly advised whenever possible. Friendship and love, both of which are essential to a happy marriage, are most likely to develop between equals ~ rather than between two people who are of a very different background.

But when both the man and the woman afford mutual pleasure to each other, and where the relatives on both sides pay respect to one another, such is called a proper connection in the proper sense of the word. Therefore a man should contract neither a high connection by which he is obliged to bow down afterwards to his kinsmen, nor a low connection, which is universally reprehended by all.

Kama Sutra

A good proposition

In the end, though, and notwithstanding everything that has already been said, a girl should always marry the man whom she likes. This is likely to be the man whom she anticipates will remain faithful to her and who is most capable of giving her the maximum pleasure. The girl who wants, above all, to be wealthy and who therefore marries a rich man without even taking any consideration of the fact that he is neither attractive nor pleasant is not likely to find happiness. Again, if a girl marries a man who already has several wives, she is unlikely to succeed in feeling very attached to him, even though he has several good qualities and is loyally obedient to her, as well as being strong, healthy, active and eager to please her. On the other hand, a husband who remains faithful to her and succeeds in remaining in firm control of himself is a much better proposition, even if he is poor as a church mouse and as ugly as sin, than a handsome man who already has several wives to his name. A man who has lost the best part of his social status and who is often away from home does not deserve to be married.

A man who is of a low mind, who has fallen from his social position, and who is much given to travelling, does not deserve to be married; neither does one who has many wives and children, or one who is devoted to sport and gambling and who comes to his wife only when he likes.

Kama Sutra

the *Virgin* bride

Before a man initiates his new wife into the delights of married life, he should first of all exercise a great deal of patience and understanding, in deference to the fact that she will probably be fearful of what lies ahead. Above all, he must try to encourage confidence in her.

Although they are now married and the girl has come to live in his house with him, she should not be expected to perform her wifely duties just yet, because she is still likely to be fearful of what lies ahead. An attempt must therefore be made to make her relax and to create confidence in her. For this reason, sex is absolutely forbidden for the first three nights and the two of them should sleep on the floor chastely, side by side. They must not partake of spicy or salty food, but should rather eat honey, milk and clarified butter. Then, for an entire week, they should bathe in the river, accompanied by the sound of music, and they should dress elegantly, take their meals together and follow their everyday household routine. They should pay attention to their relatives and friends, and to those who came to witness their marriage ceremony. The girl should perform the rites of worshipping the gods by making offerings of perfume and flowers. She will probably be both modest and shy at this time, and reluctant to be alone with him, particularly at night. This is therefore the rule that everyone should follow, whatever their caste.

For the first three days after marriage, the girl and her husband should sleep on the floor, abstain from sexual pleasures, and eat their food without seasoning it either with alkali or salt. For the next seven days they should bathe amidst the sounds of auspicious musical instruments, should decorate themselves, dine together . . .

Kama Sutra

Relaxing the new bride

Then, on the night of the tenth day, the man should attempt
to speak gently to the girl, using tender words, and thereby
try to relax her and to encourage confidence in her. Any
behaviour that she might find too abrupt from a man whom
at this stage she barely knows might cause her to become
withdrawn and to react against anything connected with the
male sex and with the things that she imagines he wants her
to do with him. As a result, some people think it is better if
he does not speak to her at all for the first three days and
remains patiently quiet. Others, on the other hand, are of the
opinion that, if he remains silent and she sees him lying as
motionless as a corpse, she may soon become so dejected
that she may assume him to be either homosexual or
impotent and may therefore look down on him as a useless
eunuch or a complete idiot. She may even consider his
reluctance to make advances to her as an insult. To force
himself on her would be a terrifying experience for her ~
that goes without saying ~ but to ignore her could be worse.

*On the night of the tenth day the man should begin in a lonely
place with soft words, and thus create confidence in the girl. Some
authors say that for the purpose of winning her over he should not
speak to her for three days, but . . . the girl may be discouraged by
seeing him spiritless like a pillar, and becoming dejected she may
begin to despise him as an eunuch.*

Kama Sutra

Gentle love games

Vatsyayana says that the man should begin to try to win the girl over and to create confidence in her, and that the way in which he should do this is with gentle, playful amorous games. That said, though, women are of a tender nature and want slow and gentle beginnnings. A rough or forcible approach would therefore be self-defeating. The man must not threaten to break her vow of chastity, as this would be to deny her belief in the importance of her virtuous conduct. Thus he must show interest in her, but he must be careful to do this without being too pushy or insistent, both of which could have the opposite effect of frightening her away and causing her to develop an instinctive hostility to any sign of affection that he makes towards her. He must understand that she can all too easily be terrified by a man whom she hardly knows, and he must treat her accordingly. This is especially so at night, when she probably feels most homesick and misses her dear ones. A woman is fragile, like a flower, and must be treated respectfully and gently until she has the confidence that she feels safe.

Vatsyayana says that the man should begin to win her over, and to create confidence in her, but should abstain at first from sexual pleasures. Women, being of a tender nature, want tender beginnings, and when they are forcibly approached by men with whom they are but slightly acquainted, they sometimes suddenly become haters . . . of the male sex.

Kama Sutra

A first embrace

A man needs to exercise a well-developed sense of discretion
and delicacy in his approaches to the girl. When he senses
that his gentle words and his games have succeeded in
making her feel sufficiently relaxed and well disposed towards
him, he can pluck up courage and risk attempting a first
embrace. This initial contact should be of the kind that she
likes most. It should be tender and he should not let it last
too long, as she will allow it only for a brief moment before
she starts to resist him. In order to avoid offending her, he
should embrace only the upper part of her body, above her
navel, as this is simpler and easier, as well as being all she will
allow at this stage. If he tries to touch the lower part of her
body, she is bound to object. If the girl is adult, or if he
already knows her, he can risk making his approaches with
the light on, but if he hardly knows her, or if she is still very
young, he should do it in the dark. Darkness is more
appropriate than blazing lights for a girl who is shy and
modest, and who is therefore all too easily frightened.

*He should embrace her with the upper part of his body, because
that is easier and simple. If the girl is grown up, or if the man has
known her for some time, he may embrace her by the light of a lamp,
but if he is not well acquainted with her, or if she is a young girl, he
should embrace her in darkness.*

Kama Sutra

If the girl allows the man to embrace her, he should offer her
a betel nut and some betel leaves, which he keeps in his
mouth. If she refuses, he will try to convince her to let him
do it by using persuasive words, sweet talk and promises and,
if all else fails, by falling at her feet. For it is a universal rule
that, no matter how embarrassed or angry a woman may be,
she can never ignore a man who is kneeling at her feet.
When he takes the betel from his mouth and puts it in hers,
he should kiss her mouth gently at the same time. If she
allows him to kiss her, he can persuade her to talk to him.
When he asks her if she wants him and whether she likes
him, she should remain silent for a while and then give him
a favourable reply by nodding her head. He should stay close
to her and offer her betel nuts, ointment and garlands of
flowers, until she speaks to him. Then, as her confidence
grows, he can touch her breasts and press them with his nails.

*When the girl accepts the embrace, the man should put a
'tambula' or screw of betel nut and betel leaves in her mouth, and if
she will not take it, he should induce her to do so by conciliatory words,
entreaties, oaths, and kneeling at her feet, for . . . a woman . . . never
disregards a man's kneeling at her feet.*

Kama Sutra

A gentle touch

If the girl tries to prevent him doing this, he should tell her
that he will not do it again as long as she will embrace him.
This should cause her to allow him to embrace her and,
while they are embracing, he should pass his hands
repeatedly over her body and place her on his lap. If she will
still not yield to him, he may frighten her by threatening to
bite and scratch her again on her lips and breasts, and to
make marks on his own body, which he will then tell people
were her doing. Her fear and confidence will probably grow
at the same rate, and the man should succeed in winning her
over to his wishes. On the second and third nights, as her
confidence continues to grow, he should pass his hands across
her entire body and kiss her all over, though he should still
not seek intercourse straight away. He should put his hands
on her thighs and between her legs, and massage them. If she
tries to stop him doing this, he should ask her what harm
there is in it and should persuade her to let him go further.
He should then loosen her clothes, untie her girdle and
touch her private parts.

*On the second and third nights, after her confidence has
increased still more, he should feel the whole of her body with his
hands, and kiss her all over; he should also place his hands upon her
thighs and shampoo them, and if he succeeds in this he should then
shampoo the joints of her thighs.*

Kama Sutra

~ *the virgin bride* ~ 75

A middle course

A man should teach her the sixty-four arts and tell her how much he loves her. He should also promise to be faithful to her and dispel any fear that she may have regarding rival women. At last, once he has overcome her shyness, he should be able to enjoy her in such a way as not to frighten her any more. A man who acts according to the inclinations of the girl should succeed in winning her confidence and she is bound to love him. A man succeeds neither by acceding to her every wish nor by opposing them, but rather by adopting a middle course. He who understands how to make a woman fall in love with him while also increasing her honour and thereby her confidence in him will soon gain her love. But he who dismisses a girl as being too timid will soon come to be despised by her as a beast who understands nothing of the female mind. A girl who is forced to succumb against her will soon becomes fearful, and will start to hate either all men, or at least her own man, with the result that she will turn to other men.

A man acting according to the inclinations of a girl should try and gain her over so that she may love him and place her confidence in him ... He who knows how to make himself beloved by women, as well as to increase their honour and create confidence in them, this man becomes an object of their love.

Kama Sutra

acts of love

People come in all sorts of shapes and sizes, and this also applies to their sexual organs. It is important to take account not only of the similarities between people but also of their differences, as these are likely to have a profound effect on the success or otherwise of a couple's sexual union.

Sexual characteristics

People do not all look the same: they come in different sizes and they have different characteristics. This doesn't just apply to their noses, or their mouths, or their chins; it applies, too, to their sexual characteristics. Therefore men and women can both be separated into three quite different types, according to the size of their sexual organs. This can have an important bearing on their sexual enjoyment. It determines, for a start, just how successful a sexual relationship between two people is likely to be. It also dictates what sort of lovemaking would be best for them. Let us look, to start with, at a man's sexual profile. Man is divided into three classes, according to the size of his penis. These are: the hare man, the bull man, and the horse man. The hare man has the smallest penis; the bull man has one of medium size; and the horse man has the largest dimensions. Similarly, the woman can also be divided into three different classes according to the depth of her vagina. These are: the deer woman, the mare woman, and the elephant woman. The deer woman has the shallowest vagina; the mare woman has one of medium size; and the elephant woman has the largest dimensions.

Men are divided into three classes: the hare man, the bull man, and the horse man, according to the size of his lingam. Women are also classed, according to the depth of her yoni, as either a female deer, a female mare, or a female elephant.

Kama Sutra

Nine potential unions

It therefore follows that there are, in all, nine possible sexual
unions between a man and a woman, according to their size.
These include three equal unions between persons who are
of similar and corresponding dimensions. These are ~ it goes
without saying ~ the very best unions of all, to which
everyone, needless to say, aspires. The equal unions, then,
which are obviously the most desirable ones, are those
between the hare and the deer; the bull and the mare; and
the horse and the elephant. In addition to these, there are
also six unequal unions, of varying inequality, which are
those between people whose dimensions simply do not
correspond. The unequal unions are those between the hare
and the mare; the hare and the elephant; the bull and the
deer; the bull and the elephant; the horse and the deer; and
the horse and the mare. These are obviously all things to be
taken into consideration when assessing the desirability of a
relationship with a particular partner or spouse, as it can have
a dramatic effect on a sexual relationship between two
people and can actually do much to make or break its
chances of success or otherwise.

*There are thus three equal unions between persons of
corresponding dimensions, and there are six unequal unions, when the
dimensions do not correspond, or nine in all. The equal unions are:
hare/deer; bull/mare; horse/elephant. The unequal unions are:
hare/mare; hare/elephant; bull/deer; bull/elephant; horse/deer;
horse/mare.*

Kama Sutra

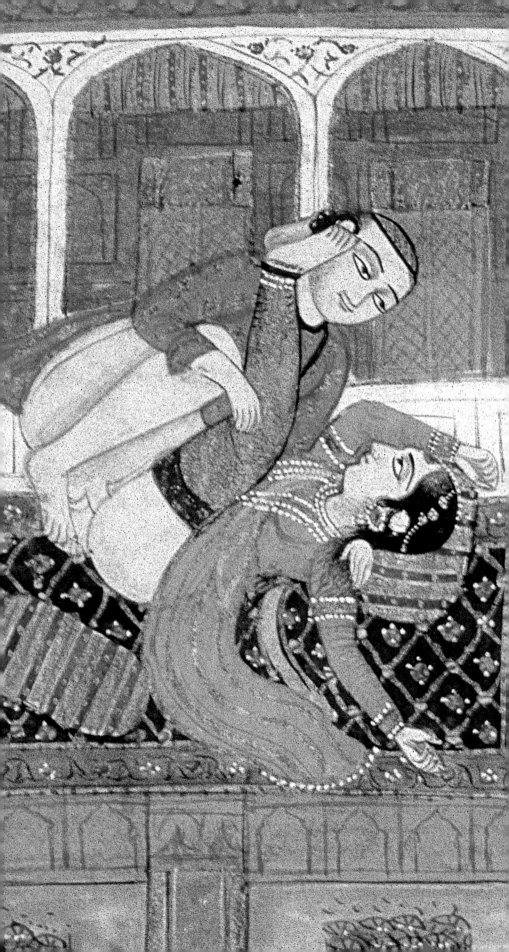

Unequal unions

In unions that are considered to be unequal, where the male exceeds the female in terms of size, his union with a woman who is immediately next to him in size is called a high union, and is of two kinds, while his union with a woman who is most remote from him in size, on the other hand, is called a low union and is of one kind only. In other words, both the horse and the mare, and the bull and the deer form a high union, while the horse and the deer form the highest union of all. Of all the possible unequal unions, the coupling of extremes ~ in other words the highest and the lowest ~ is quite definitely the worst. Anything that comes in between is middling. High unions are generally better than low ones, because they generally allow the male to satisfy his own passions without injuring the female, while in the latter it is difficult for the female to be satisfied by any means.

In these unequal unions, when the male exceeds the female in point of size, his union with a woman who is immediately next to him in size is called high union, and is of two kinds; while his union with the woman most remote from him in size is called the highest union, and is of one kind only.

Kama Sutra

Similarly, the situation is just the same when the roles are reversed. In unions that are considered to be unequal, where the female exceeds the male in terms of size, her union with a man who is immediately next to her in size is called a low union, and is of two kinds, while her union with a man who is most remote from her in size, on the other hand, is called the lowest union and is of one kind only. Thus, on the female side, the elephant and the bull, and the mare and the hare form low unions, while the elephant and the hare form the lowest union. Whether it is the male or the female who is superior doesn't really matter, though high unions are usually better than low ones. The most important lesson to be learned from this is that it is always the coupling of extremes ~ in other words of the highest and the lowest together ~ which is quite definitely the worst of all possible unions.

On the other hand, when the female exceeds the male in point of size, her union with a man immediately next to her in size is called low union; and is of two kinds; while her union with a man most remote from her in size is called the lowest union, and is of one kind only.

Kama Sutra

The force of passion

As well as differences in size, there are also differences in the force of passion or carnal desire, and these can be just as important. Just as there are nine different kinds of union in terms of size, so there are nine different kinds of union in terms of passion. The three equal unions are when both partners have a similarly small, middling or intense force of passion. The unequal unions are when both partners have different forces of passion ~ in other words, one has a small passion and the other has a middling one; or one has a small passion and the other has an intense one; or one has an intense passion and the other has a middling one. A man is called a man of small passion when his desire at the time of sexual intercourse is not great, whose semen is scanty, or who cannot tolerate the warm embraces of the woman. Those who are known as having an intense passion are full of desire, and those who fall somewhere between the two are known as men of middling passion. Similarly, women are also supposed to be subject to the three degrees of feeling as detailed above.

There are also nine kinds of union according to the force of passion or carnal desire. The three equal unions are when both partners have either small, middling or intense passion. The unequal unions are small/middling; small/intense; middling/small; middling/intense; intense/small; and intense/middling.

Kama Sutra

A question of time

There are also nine kinds of union in terms of time: there are those who take only a short time before they come, those who take a moderate time, and those who take a long time. It is therefore not always possible for a couple to reach orgasm at the same time, and this can be quite a problem. It is important to realize, too, that women do not ejaculate in the same way as men. In men, ejaculation brings an end to their desire, while women feel a certain pleasure but they do not want to stop as men do. So if a man takes a long time until he reaches orgasm, the woman loves him all the more, whereas if he comes too quickly she will be dissatisfied because she will not manage to experience pleasure. A man ejaculates at the end of intercourse, whereas the woman's desire does not cease when he has achieved orgasm. Her enjoyment is continual and her need for a man carries on even after she has achieved orgasm. During intercourse, the friction of the man's penis may calm her excitement, but it is in the signs of affection, such as kissing and caressing, that she finds the greatest pleasure.

How someone may ask here: if men and women are beings of the same kind, and are engaged in bringing about the same result, why should they have different works to do. Vatsyayana says that this is so because the ways of working as well as the consciousness of pleasure in men and women are different.

Kama Sutra

Human beings

When a man and a woman unite for the same purpose, which is the pursuit of pleasure, it would be wrong to assume that the pleasure that they obtain is in any way different. Men and women are both human beings and the pleasure that they seek is therefore the same. There is no difference in the aim, only in the way in which they achieve it and in how long this takes. Just as there are nine kinds of union with regard to the dimensions of the sexual organs, to the force of passion and to the time that is spent, so the possible permutations of all these factors are endless, producing innumerable kinds of different union. Men should therefore use the techniques that they deem to be most suitable for each occasion. At the first lovemaking, from the beginning of the act until orgasm, a man's ardour is so strong that he tries to get to his conclusion as quickly as possible. The second time, however, he takes a long time to reach orgasm, which suits a woman's needs. Her reactions are different: her first orgasm is slow and lasts a short time; the second is quick and lasts much longer.

At the first time of sexual union the passion of the male is intense, and his time is short, but in subsequent unions . . . the reverse of this is the case. With the female however it is the contrary, for at the first time her passion is weak, and then her time long, but on subsequent occasions . . . her passion is intense and her time short . . .

Kama Sutra

forbidden fruits

There were certain sexual practices, such as cunnilingus and fellatio, which were normally forbidden in those days between a husband and wife. In spite of this ~ or perhaps because of it ~ some people were only too prepared to seek out these pleasures at virtually any cost.

Pleasures such as cunnilingus and fellatio were forbidden
between husband and wife and were therefore practised by
the third sex, or eunuchs. There were two different kinds of
eunuch, who were also described as neuter. There were those
who maintained a male appearance, and who had
moustaches, body hair and so on. And then there were those
who had a female appearance, who had breasts, wore
women's clothes, did their hair in a feminine style and
behaved in a characteristically feminine way, marked by silly
giggling, flirting and modesty. Prostitutes who belonged to
the third sex were known as catamites. Those who had the
appearance of women performed a special sexual act, for
which they used their mouth between the thighs of the man.
This act was known, for obvious reasons, as superior coition,
and these eunuchs earned their living from offering this form
of eroticism to those who wanted it. It was known as
auparishtaka, or fellatio. They led the life of courtesans,
making themselves available to men who demanded this sort
of erotic favour.

*There are two kinds of eunuchs, those that are disguised as males,
and those that are disguised as females. Eunuchs disguised as
females imitate their dress, speech, gesture, tenderness, timidity,
simplicity, softness and bashfulness. The acts that are done on the
jaghana or middle parts of women, are done in the mouths of these
eunuchs, and this is called Auparishtaka.*

Kama Sutra

The role of eunuchs

But there are also eunuchs who are prepared to perform these intimate acts of oral sex for men. These eunuchs who have a preference for sex with men but who keep this fact carefully hidden from the world are very careful to maintain their appearance in front of everyone as a man. These people earn their living outwardly rather as hairdressers or masseurs, devoting all their energies to massaging the limbs of their clients. They, too, practise oral sex, but there is nothing straightforward or open about what they intend to do and, as their sexual desires are hidden, a man who comes to see them cannot be sure of reaching his goal with them. While such a eunuch is seemingly intent on massaging a man, he embraces the man's thighs and draws them closer to his face as he concentrates on stroking, kneading and pummelling them, and then gently touches the sexual area that lies at the joints of the man's thighs, including his ass and his testicles.

Eunuchs disguised as males keep their desires secret, and when they wish to do anything they lead the life of shampooers. Under the pretence of shampooing, a eunuch of this kind embraces and draws towards himself the thighs of the man whom he is shampooing, and after this he touches the joints of his thighs and his jaghana or central portion of his body.

Kama Sutra

Then, when the eunuch has succeeded in causing the man to have an erection, which he obviously takes as indicative of the man's desire for congress with him, the eunuch takes the man's penis in his hands and proceeds to stroke and rub it triumphantly. He laughs delightedly at the fact that the man has managed to get himself into this state and that his penis had become erect even though he has not even touched it yet, and pretends to mock him for this, but he does not, as yet, do anything that will cause him to ejaculate. If the man does not tell the eunuch to continue, even though he is by now aware of the eunuch's sexual intentions, then the eunuch will carry on of his own accord and begins to suck on his own initiative. If, on the other hand, the man indicates his desire for the eunuch to suck his penis, the eunuch will make a show of protesting and will refuse to do as he is asked, at least for a while, though eventually, of course, he will give in enthusiastically and be only too willing to perform oral sex on the man.

Then, if he finds the lingam of the man erect, he presses it with his hands, and chaffs him for getting into that state. If, after this, and after knowing the eunuch's intention, the man does not tell the eunuch to proceed, then the latter does it of his own accord and begins the congress.

Kama Sutra

Different kinds of fellatio

There are eight different ways in which the eunuch can perform this kind of oral sex. These are as follows: the nominal congress; nibbling the sides; the outside pressing; the inside pressing; kissing; rubbing; sucking a mango fruit; and swallowing it up. The nominal congress is when the eunuch holds the man's penis in one hand, bends down to place it in his mouth, rounding his lips over the end of the penis, while moving it around in his mouth. Nibbling the sides is when he covers the end of the man's penis with his fingertips bunched together like a flowerbud and presses the sides of the penis with his lips, while nibbling at them slightly at the same time with his teeth. As soon as he has done this, he immediately softens his bite and allows the penis to calm down. As he does each of these in turn, the eunuch expresses his desire to rest, but each time the man pleads with him to continue and to do the next thing on the agenda . . . and so on until, in the end, he achieves the fulfilment of his desire.

When, holding the man's lingam with his hand, and placing it between his lips, the eunuch moves about his mouth, it is called the 'nominal congress'. When, covering the end of the lingam with his fingers collected together like the bud of a plant or flower, the eunuch presses the sides of it with his lips, using his teeth also, it is called 'biting the sides'.

Kama Sutra

Feverish pitch

By now, the man has been aroused to a feverish pitch by the eunuch who is nibbling his penis. He then asks the eunuch to proceed to the next contact between penis and lips. This is known as the outside pressing, which is when the eunuch brings his mouth close to the erect penis and, allowing it to enter his mouth, presses down on it with his lips while kissing it and, at the same time, sucking hard, before eventually letting go and releasing it. The inside pressing is always done on the client's request, when he is really excited and is on the point of orgasm. He then promises to pay the eunuch, who allows the penis to enter further into his mouth and presses the end between his lips while sucking gently, causing his client to emit a little liquid from the end. The next stage is kissing, which is when the eunuch seizes the penis with his hand, rather than his lips, exposes the head and kisses it. This is known as the kissing hold.

When, being desired to proceed, the eunuch presses the end of the lingam with his lips closed together, and kisses it as if he were drawing it out, it is called the 'outside pressing'. When, being asked to go on, he puts the lingam further into his mouth, and presses it with his lips and then takes it out, it is called the 'inside pressing'.

Kama Sutra

Tongue pressure

Then comes the stage in the process known as rubbing, or browsing, which is when the eunuch licks the penis all over with the tip of his tongue in the kissing hold, and flicks his tongue tantalizingly over the sensitive little opening. In order to do what is known as sucking the mango, the eunuch exposes the head of the penis and puts it halfway into his mouth, while both pressing it passionately with the base of his tongue and sucking hard, an action that is rather similar to what one does with one's mouth when trying to extract the juice of a mango ~ hence its name. Finally, when the eunuch has understood that his client is ready to reach his climax, he puts the whole penis in his mouth and makes him come with the pressure of his tongue against the head of his penis. This causes a dramatic gushing of sperm and the eunuch continues to press hard on his penis, right up until the end. This is known as swallowing it up, or devouring, and marks the high point of the process of oral coition.

When, in the same way, he puts the half of it into his mouth and forcibly kisses and sucks it, this is called 'sucking a mango fruit'. And lastly, when, with the consent of the man, the eunuch puts the whole lingam into his mouth, and presses it to the very end, as if he were going to swallow it up, it is called 'swallowing it up'.

Kama Sutra

In some cases it is the young male servants ~ who wear bright, glittering rings in their ears ~ who perform oral sex with their masters. It is also practised by some citizens who know each other well and who trust each other implicitly, among themselves. Some of the women of the harem also perform oral sex on each other's vulvas, and there are also some men who do the same thing with women and who instinctively know how to kiss the vulva from their experience of kissing the mouth. Sometimes, a man and a woman practise inverse coition, she sucking his penis and he licking her vulva simultaneously. When a man and a woman lie down together in this way, in an inverted position, to practise this kind of inverse congress, it is known as the congress of the crow. Like crows, the man and woman peck at each other, each seizing the other one's sex in their mouths and drinking each other's secretions in their ardour. This is considered an acceptable practice between partners of the same social standing, but it is not recommended with people of other castes. Acts between equals are always better.

Some women of the harem, when they are amorous, do the acts of the mouth on the yonis of one another, and some men do the same thing with women . . . When a man and woman lie down in an inverted order, with the head of the one towards the feet of the other and carry on this congress, it is called the 'congress of a crow'.

Kama Sutra

pain
and
pleasure

Forms of manual contact, such as embraces, kisses, scratches, bites and blows, are all practised for the purposes of arousal. And sometimes, conducting a love affair can be rather like having a quarrel, so that violence becomes an integral part of love play.

Pressing, marking, or scratching with the nails

In the heat of passion, when lovers get carried away, the nails may be used to scratch, scrape and mark the other person's body. This is an effective way of increasing someone's level of arousal. Failing that and when enthusiasm is low, scratching can be used to demonstrate a vigorous strength of feeling. It is particularly recommended on special occasions ~ say, on the evening of an amorous encounter, or on returning from a journey, or just before setting off on a departure, or at a reconciliation with an angry lover, or perhaps when the woman is drunk ~ though it is not appropriate in every circumstance. Scratching is a sign of affection, as well as one of anger or joy, and it is a valuable token of remembrance ~ a reminder of the passage of a former love when one's lover is no longer there. Particularly good places to be pressed with the nails include the armpits, the throat, the breasts, the lips, the sexual organs, and the thighs. The qualities of good nails are that they should be bright, well set, clean, unbroken, convex, soft and glossy in appearance.

When love becomes intense, pressing with the nails or scratching the body with them is practised, and it is done on the following occasions: on the first visit; at the time of setting out on a journey; on the return from a journey; at the time when an angry lover is reconciled; and lastly when the woman is intoxicated.

Kama Sutra

~ pain and pleasure ~   *113*

Biting

All those places on the body that can be kissed may also be
bitten, with the exception of the upper lip, the tongue and
the eyes. That still leaves plenty of choice, though, including
the forehead, the lower lip, the neck, the cheeks, the chest,
the breasts, the sides of the body, and the genital region. Just
as there are particular types of nails that are regarded as good
and desirable, so this applies, too, to teeth. The qualities of
good teeth are that they should be even, bright, clean, shiny,
well-proportioned, unbroken and capable of cutting. Bad
teeth, on the other hand, are blunt, rough, soft, large, loose
and stick out from the gums. Different regions have different
habits when it comes to scratching and biting, but it is more
important to follow one's inclinations than to obey local
customs. A passionate woman glues her lips to her lover's and
forces him to lie down. Then she covers his entire body with
bites ~ biting him wherever he has bitten her ~ like a
lunatic, and rejoices at the efforts he makes to get away from
her. She embraces him with such force that their two bodies
become one single body. In this way, if men and women act
according to each other's liking, their love for one another
will be no less, even after one hundred years.

*All the places that can be kissed, are also the places that can be
bitten, except the upper lip, the interior of the mouth, and the eyes. The
qualities of good teeth are as follows: they should be equal, possessed
of a pleasing brightness, capable of being coloured, of proper
proportions, unbroken, and with sharp ends.*

Kama Sutra

Not to everyone's taste

Forms of manual contact, such as embraces, kisses, scratches, bites and blows, are all practised for the purposes of arousal. There are, it should be understood, areas where the population is mainly Aryan and where the women do not care for injuries to be inflicted on their bodies by a man's nails or teeth. It should not be thought, therefore, that the practices which are described here will be to everyone's taste, nor that they will be acceptable anywhere in the world. There are ten different kinds of possible bite and a woman wears these marks for all to see. Some bites are more obvious than others, either because they are more or less vivid, or because of where they are situated on the body. The visible signs of biting vary, for example, from a faint necklace of dots on the forehead or the thighs, to a circle of small, irregular tooth marks known as a scattered cloud beneath the breasts. They are a sign of a man's possession which a woman wears with pride. They are an indication that a woman is truly loved and has been lustily desired.

The marking with the nails, and the biting of the following things: an ornament of the forehead, an ear ornament, a bunch of flowers, a betel leaf, or a tamala leaf, which are worn by, or belong to the woman that is beloved, are signs of the desire of enjoyment.

Kama Sutra

A love quarrel

The sexual relations between two people can be thought of as a kind of quarrel, and eroticism generally as a battleground. What appears to be a conflict between the two lovers is in reality a struggle between the two of them, because both the man and the woman are forced to confront one another in order to assert themselves. This could not be done by either kindness or affection. This may be surprising because love is generally thought of as being associated with gentleness, but gentleness would not, in fact, have the desired effect. A show of cruelty, rather, is therefore essential to good intercourse and has its place in all sexual acts. There are several particularly good places for lovers to aim blows at each other. These are found on the shoulders, on the head, in the gap between the breasts, on the back, anywhere in the area of the sexual region, and on the sides of the body. As a result of the sexual interplay between lovers, the blows that a person receives there are, in fact, part of the pleasure of sexual intercourse.

Sexual intercourse can be compared to a quarrel, on account of the contrarieties of love and its tendency to dispute. The place of striking with passion is the body, and on the body the special places are:

The shoulders, the head, the space between the breasts, the back, the jaghana (or middle part of the body) and the sides.

Kama Sutra

Different ways of striking

There are, first of all, four quite different ways in which it is possible to deliver a blow to a person as part of sexual foreplay. These are the following: using the side of the hand, with the palm of the open hand, with the fist, and with the ends of the joined fingers. None of these is in the slightest difficult to master and which particular method a person chooses to use is of very little importance, because all will have much the same effect on the person who receives it. Because his violent actions cause her pain, the woman groans under his blows and, as his blows vary in their ferocity, she may also sigh. The precise kind of sound she utters will depend on the pain she feels and is thus an expression, in sound, of the pain that she experiences. Her cries may come in a range of eight different kinds, and these are described as the thundering sound, the cooing sound, the weeping sound or the sound 'Phut', all of which express a particular state of mind which is an important part of erotic aggression.

Striking is of four kinds: Striking with the back of the hand, striking with the fist, striking with the fingers a little contracted and striking with the open palm of the hand . . . On account of its causing pain, striking gives rise to the hissing sound . . . and to the eight kinds of crying . . .

Kama Sutra

Expressing her feelings

In addition to these sounds, a woman will also speak words which have a particular meaning and which express exactly how she is made to feel at the time. She may, for example, call for her mother, or she may beg for mercy, or she may plead with him to stop, or she may even, perhaps, beg him to continue ~ depending on how she feels at that particular moment. When the woman groans under the force of her lover's blows, she will utter cries that are described as being like those of the pigeon, the cuckoo, the turtle dove, the parrot, the bee, the nightingale, the goose, the duck or the partridge. A woman's sighs can be as attractive as the sound of a song. When she is sitting on his knees in anticipation of love, he should give her blows to her back with his fist and, pretending that she cannot bear this, she will cry and voice a long drawn-out 'Han' while directing angry blows at him in return for his abuse of her. But then, as she eventually begins to relax and to enjoy his blows, he should strike her progressively harder and harder, and aim some of his blows at other places, too.

Blows with the fist should be given on the back of the woman, while she is sitting on the lap of the man, and she should give blows in return, abusing the man as if she were angry, and making the cooing and the weeping sounds.

Kama Sutra

The natural world

There are all kinds of amorous practices that can be observed among quadrupeds, with the result that ~ when inspiration escapes him ~ a man can find the models for his amusement in the natural world. A man can enjoy sex , for example, with two women, both of whom love him and both of whom have similar sexual tastes. This is known as the united congress. The two women lie on the same bed and the man makes use of them both. While he is mounting one of the women, the other one kisses him and, after pleasuring one, he brings the other one expertly to orgasm. Or he may experience group sex with many different women, in which case it is known as the congress of a herd of cows, referring to the fact that the man is doing just as a bull does with his herd of cows. And other animals provide interesting models, too, in terms of their different kinds of congress. It is amusing, for example, to imitate the mating games of the elephants, which take place only in the water with many females, or those of a group of goats, or a herd of deer, and so on.

When a man enjoys two women at the same time, both of whom love him equally, it is called the 'united congress'. When a man enjoys many women altogether, it is called the 'congress of a herd of cows'.

Kama Sutra

the wives of others

It is normally forbidden to have sexual relations with women who are already married. There are, however, situations in which this is acceptable, but this needs careful thought. In the full knowledge of this, a man must obviously take care to guard his own wife.

A question of adultery

Under normal circumstances, sexual relations with women
who are already married to other men are forbidden. Such
relations will not, in any case, bring with them the joy of
having children, so the question of adultery must always be
carefully examined before it is actually committed. Adultery
with someone else's wife can sometimes be acceptable, but
only in certain circumstances. The prospect of sex with other
men's wives requires deep reflection before indulging in it.
Above all, it should not be done merely for the sake of carnal
desire, but should be resorted to only for very special reasons,
such as in extreme matters of life and death. The possibilities
of success must first be thought about carefully, and the
relative benefits and risks should be weighed up accordingly.
What will be the effects of this union? Will it be worth it?
Will it cause problems? Will the relationship last? Would life
be bearable without her? And what will be the risk to the
reputations of both parties involved if he succumbs to
temptation? Only once all these questions have been dealt
with satisfactorily can a man allow himself to take possession
of someone else's wife.

*The wives of other people may be resorted to but it must be
distinctly understood that it is only allowed for special reasons and
not for mere carnal desire. The possibility of their acquisition, their
fitness for cohabitation, the danger to oneself in uniting with them, and
the future effect of these unions, should first of all be examined.*

Kama Sutra

Weighing up the pros and cons

Before allowing himself to indulge in the desire for relations with another man's wife, he should think hard about what he stands to gain from this relationship. There are few reasons for which a man may resort to sex with someone else's wife, the most important of which is to save his own life. When he realizes that his passion is passing from one stage of intensity to another and that his passion may in the end destroy him, then ~ and only then ~ may he proceed. There are ten stages of intensity, which are distinguished by the following marks:

1. Physical attraction
2. An affinity with her personality
3. She becomes an obsession
4. An inability to sleep
5. Loss of appetite
6. A loss of interest in everything
7. No sense of propriety
8. Madness of love
9. Loss of consciousness
10. Inevitable death

When he sees the woman, the man develops a strong desire to possess her and, as he passes from one stage of desire to another, he becomes deeply affected by it. When he reaches the stage of believing that he can no longer live without her, he knows that he cannot renounce his desire for her and that he has to possess her.

A man may resort to the wife of another, for the purpose of saving his own life, when he perceives that his love for her proceeds from one degree of intensity to another.

Kama Sutra

What chance of success?

While he is thinking over the best way of implementing his plan and weighing up his chances of success, a man must reflect on what kind of woman she is. There are some men who generally obtain success with women. These are men who are well versed in the science of love, men who have secured their confidence and who send presents to them, men who talk well, men who have not loved other women previously, and men who surpass their husbands in terms of learning and good looks. There are, similarly, certain women with whom one has a particularly good chance of success. These are women who stand at the door of their houses and are always looking out at the street, and women who are always staring at you, particularly when they indulge in sideways glances. Moreover and in particular, look out for a woman whose husband has taken another wife without good reason, a woman who dresses scantily at parties, a woman who hates her husband or is hated by him, a woman who has no children, a poor woman who is fond of parties, and a woman whose husband is away a lot.

Desire, which springs from nature, and which is increased by art, and from which all danger is taken away by wisdom, becomes firm and secure. A clever man, depending on his own ability, and observing carefully the ideas and thoughts of women, and removing the causes of their turning away from men, is generally successful with them.

Kama Sutra

State of mind

When a man is trying to seduce a women, he should try to understand her state of mind, and there are certain signs that will help him do this. If she seems to be paying him attention but does not actually make her own intentions clear, then his best chances of success are to find someone who will act as a go-between for him. If she meets him once and then turns up for a second meeting looking even lovelier than the first time, then he can be sure that she will be his. A woman who teases a man shamelessly ~ by appearing to let him have his way with her to start with and then changing her mind ~ should not be taken seriously, though only time will tell what she will choose to do in the end. Be wary, too, of any woman who makes every effort to avoid the attentions of a man and refuses resolutely to meet him, though a clever go-between may succeed in swaying her. When a woman makes a show of reprimanding a man while at the same time acting affectionately towards him, he can be quite sure that she will be his.

A woman who meets a man in lonely places, and puts up with the touch of his foot, but pretends, because of the indecision of her mind, not to be aware of it, should be conquered by patience, and by continued efforts . . . When a woman gives a man an opportunity, and makes her own love manifest to him, he should proceed to enjoy her.

Kama Sutra

The royal harem

The ladies of the royal harem have no difficulty in getting young citizens into their apartments. They are sometimes introduced into the harem dressed as women, accompanied by the maidservants. In order to be let in and out again, they distribute tips to the women who guard the entrance, and who are thus able to derive some profit from their visits. The palace is huge and the guards are careless and inattentive, so it is not usually difficult to get in. This generally takes place when provisions are being delivered to the palace, or when things are being taken out of it, or when drinking festivals are going on, or when the female attendants are in a hurry, or when people are out on a country excursion, or when the King is absent on a long pilgrimage and has left his queens in the palace. A citizen should always be careful, though, as there is a great risk involved to his life if he is caught. He should enter only if he is sure of the way out. Anyone who finds it easy to get in and out should take advantage of this and take the opportunity to come in at every opportunity ~ perhaps even every day.

By means of their female attendants the ladies of the royal harem generally get men into their apartments in the disguise or dress of women. Their female attendants and the daughters of their nurses, who are acquainted with their secrets, should exert themselves to get men to come to the harem in this way . . .

Kama Sutra

United they stand . . .

The women living in the harem are familiar with each other's
secrets and know everything there is to know about each
other. If one of the women in the harem decides to act on her
own initiative and to allow herself a special adventure quite
apart from the others ~ special precisely because it is forbidden
~ she then separates herself from the others. This is a mistake
and it carries enormous risks. It is a dangerous enterprise
because the other women may become angry at her secret
behaviour, which they regard as treachery, and denounce her to
the King. This will not happen, though, when all the women
of the harem participate in each other's actions. Sharing their
acts, their secrets, their thoughts in this way means that all the
women have but one aim in common and they therefore help
each other. This binds them together. If one of them is accused
of bad behaviour, this inevitably reflects on all the other
women living with her in the harem, so it is safest for everyone
concerned if they all share in each other's activities and in this
way stick together. Thus secrets are kept by the whole harem
and no one is exposed. United they stand, divided they fall.

*The women of the royal harem know each other's secrets, and having
but one object to attain, they give assistance to each other. A young man,
who enjoys all of them, and who is common to them all, can continue
enjoying his union with them so long as it is kept quiet . . .*

Kama Sutra

Guarding his own wife

A man can learn a lot from the behaviour of the women in the royal harem, and he should understand how important it is to guard his own wife. The followers of Babhravya say that a man should cause his wife to associate with a young woman, who will then be sure to tell him any of his wife's secrets that he should know, as well as any relevant information regarding his wife's chastity. But Vatsyayana disagrees with this. He says that a man should not immediately punish a woman who may not actually be guilty, nor should he accuse her without understanding the reasons for her behaviour. A man should not cause his innocent wife to be corrupted by bringing her into the company of a woman who is prepared to deceive her in this way. He should consider, rather, the reasons for a woman's misconduct ~ such as too many parties, the husband's misconduct, uncontrolled relations with the husband's brothers, a husband's repeated absences, his many trips abroad, lack of money and the company of loose women. A man who has thoroughly studied the parts of the *Kama Sutra* concerning sexual relations with other men's wives and who has developed an understanding of these matters should not, if he is intelligent, be deceived by his own wives.

Thus act the wives of others. For these reasons a man should guard his own wife . . . A clever man, learning from the Shastras the ways of winning over the wives of other people, is never deceived in the case of his own wives.

Kama Sutra

the life of a wife

A wife must be attentive to her husband's wishes at all times, particularly if she is his only wife. If he has several of them, this may cause potential problems, and a wife should be careful in her behaviour towards her husband's other wives.

The role of the wife

A girl should marry a man who is at least three years older than she is and who is neither superior nor inferior to her, but is from her own circle and therefore of broadly equal status to hers. Equality is a prerequisite of a happy marriage, and a couple should enjoy the same pleasures, tastes, pastimes and interests. That said, a girl who has many suitors, all of whom are eager to marry her, should only wed a man whom she likes, who she thinks will be obedient and faithful to her, and who she thinks will be able to give her pleasure. That a couple should afford mutual sexual pleasure to one another is absolutely essential if the relationship is to be a lasting one. Once the girl is married to the man, she may either be the only wife, or she may be one of several wives, and this will, of course, affect the role she is required to play in his life. The wife who is the only one trusts and loves her husband, has a place for him in her heart as a god, and is utterly devoted to him. The wife who is one wife among several should, ideally, do the same, but this may be rather more difficult because there is always a risk of potentially unpleasant situations.

A girl who is much sought after should marry the man that she likes, and who she thinks would be obedient to her, and capable of giving her pleasure.

Kama Sutra

Marrying for love

A young woman should marry out of love and never from a desire for wealth without first taking into account the character or looks of the man concerned. The wives of rich men, especially where men have chosen to have many wives, do not in general become unduly attached to their husbands and may not even remain loyal to them. Even though such a wife may appear to have all the outward trappings of a contented married life, she may nevertheless not be happy, in which case she may still be obliged to have recourse to other men for solace and physical pleasure. When she is alone with her husband, she should serve him well and should not tell him of the pain that she suffers as a result of there being a rival wife. An even-tempered woman who conducts herself according to the principles of the holy scriptures will succeed in winning her husband's attachment and may thus obtain a superiority over her rivals. She should never reveal her love for her husband, nor his love for her, to anyone else, whether tempted to do this out of pride or anger, because a man will despise a wife who dares to reveal any of his secrets.

The wives of rich men, where there are many wives, are not generally attached to their husbands, and are not confidential with them, and even though they possess all the external enjoyments of life, still have recourse to other men.

Kama Sutra

Submissive and respectful

The wife should always welcome any of her husband's
friends with flower garlands, sandalwood incense, and betel,
as is the custom in every well-kept house. She should be
submissive and respectful in her relations with her in-laws,
and should take care to agree with whatever pleases them
and never to contradict them. She should buy earthenware,
bamboo, wooden, leather, iron and copper utensils cheaply,
and she should buy salt, oil and spices, all of which she keeps
in special containers, while she hides the pots containing rare
products. She must make sure that the servants do their work
properly and she must regulate her spending by calculating
her annual income and keeping accounts of all her entries
and expenses. She should take care to busy herself at all times
by making butter with leftover milk, preparing molasses with
sugarcane and oil with colza, spinning cotton and making
cloth with the thread, and setting aside the rice water, wheat
bran and burned charcoal for re-use. She should make sure,
too, that she lays in stocks of wine in jars and jars of liquors,
ready whenever they are needed. She should not laugh too
loudly, which would be vulgar, and she must not become
overly excited at amusements and games.

*In her relations with her father-in-law and mother-in-law, she
must be submissive and not contradict them, speak gently in front of
them and not laugh too loudly, show that she agrees with what pleases
them and, as far as what displeases them, act so as not to contradict
them.*

Kama Sutra

In charge of the household

A virtuous wife will conform to her husband's every wish.
With her husband's consent, she takes responsibility for the
household and involves herself entirely in its domestic tasks.
She attends to cleaning the clothes, tidying the house, doing
the flower arrangements, cleaning the floor and making
herself attractive to see at all times. She also performs the
three important daily rites of offering to the gods and
worshipping them at their domestic shrine. She must sow the
seeds on carefully prepared ground, in well-ordered rows, for
aromatic plants such as coriander, ginger and jasmine, and for
vegetables such as spinach and fennel. She must avoid all
contact with beggars, female Buddhist mendicants, unchaste
women, fortune-tellers or witches. She should always prepare
the foods and drinks that she knows her husband to like best.
And when she hears his voice outside, she should welcome
her husband home, always radiant, smiling, elegantly dressed
and wearing all her jewels, with the words, "What are your
orders?' – prepared, as always, to obey his every wish. She
must observe the signs, however small, that enable her to
guess what he desires. When she sends the servants away and
the two are finally alone, she will bow at her husband's feet.
And she must fall asleep after him and wake before him.

*A virtuous woman, who has affection for her husband, should act
in conformity with his wishes as if he were a divine being, and with
his consent should take upon herself the whole care of his family. She
should keep the whole house well cleaned, and arrange flowers of
various kinds in different parts of it . . .*

Kama Sutra

Her husband's welfare

The devoted wife will do everything she can for the promotion of her husband's welfare. This is the case irrespective of her background, her history or her past. She may be from a noble highborn family; or she may have married in her infancy and been widowed young before even arriving at puberty, and then remarried afterwards; or she may even be an ex-concubine. None of this matters. Whatever her origins and whatever her past, she now wishes to tend to the well-being of her husband above all things and will therefore lead an absolutely irreproachable life. Women who act in this way are protected by their good conduct and will thus be able to acquire the three principal aims of life that everyone strives for. These are Dharma (the practice of virtue, spiritualism and such conduct as is required by the teachings of the scriptures), Artha (the acquisition of material wealth) and Kama (love, eroticism and the consciousness of the pleasures of the five senses, all of which are learned with the help of the *Kama Sutra*). Their exemplary behaviour will keep their husbands devoted to them, which will give them, in turn, the desirable social status as a single wife, without the threat of having to compete with other, rival wives.

The wife, whether she be a woman of noble family, or a virgin widow remarried, or a concubine, should lead a chaste life, devoted to her husband, and doing everything for his welfare. Women acting thus acquire Dharma, Artha, and Kama, obtain a high position, and generally keep their husbands devoted to them.

Kama Sutra

An absent husband

When her husband embarks on a journey to distant climes, his wife should spend her time on her own. She should wear neither any of the signs of marriage nor her jewellery, and should spend her time attending to the worship of the gods, praying and fasting. She must also pass the hours looking after the house, performing all the daily tasks that her husband has taught her to do. She will sleep beside her parents-in-law and do as they tell her. Her occupations during this time will include parties for the children, and checking the accounts. She will only go to visit her family in case of sickness or bereavement or for a religious festival, and she will always be accompanied at such times by members of her husband's family, who will stand witness to the respectability of her visit. She must not stay away long, for fear of annoying her parents-in-law, and will never go out except when she is accompanied. When her husband returns from his trip, she must remain in the garments that she has been wearing during his absence and must be careful not to make herself too beautiful. She and her husband will worship the gods together, and after that she will welcome him home.

When her husband departs on a journey abroad, she removes the married woman's marks and her jewels, dedicates herself to devotion, and looks after the house according to the rules established by her husband.

Kama Sutra

A strict hierarchy

When there are many wives, there is a strict hierarchy
between them which they should always observe. The eldest
wife should offer help and advice to the younger ones, who
should all treat each other's children as if they were their
own. The eldest wife should associate with the one who is
immediately next to her in both rank and age. She should
provoke a quarrel between the wife who has until recently
been the husband's favourite and his current favourite. She
should make the favourite wife out to be a nasty, scheming
woman, while not looking as if any of this was her doing.
She should also try to cause a quarrel between the favourite
wife and her husband and, if it looks as though her husband
still loves his favourite wife, she should make a point of
trying to bring about a reconciliation between the two of
them, which will put her in her husband's good books. The
youngest wife should respect the oldest wife as her mother,
and should not tell anyone anything about their household
without the oldest wife's permission. She should care for the
children of the older wives even more than for her own.

*When there are many other wives besides herself ... the younger
wife should regard the elder wife of her husband as her mother, and
should not give anything away, even to her own relations, without her
knowledge. She should tell her everything about herself, and not
approach her husband without her permission.*

Kama Sutra

the life
of a
courtesan

Just as a wife, a courtesan
should also be aware at all times
of her duties and responsibilities.
Every self-respecting courtesan
should observe a strict code of
conduct, both for her own success
in life and for her own happiness.

Pleasure and money

By sleeping with a man, a courtesan gains both pleasure from the sexual act, as well as money and therefore her means of subsistence. She lives on the money that she receives. Pleasure is her livelihood and she sells it for money. In order to obtain the money, the erotic attraction may be either real or simulated. When her desire for a man is genuine and is stronger than her desire for money, the act of love is a spontaneous one and its pleasure is immediate. But when her desire for money predominates over her love of him, her desire is feigned and she will not experience real pleasure. In this case, however, she must nevertheless pretend that she is truly enamoured of her lover and it is important that she makes him believe this. In order to entrap him, she must not talk only of money. She will entrap him, rather, by appearing to be more interested in him than in money. She must make him believe that her desire is genuine and in this way it appears natural for her to receive a gratification. She must never give sexual favours without being paid for it. She must affirm her power and she must never neglect her interests.

By having intercourse with men, courtesans obtain sexual pleasure, as well as their own maintenance. Now, when a courtesan takes up with a man from love, the action is natural; but when she resorts to him for the purpose of getting money, her action is artificial or forced.

Kama Sutra

Looking good

A courtesan must always be elegantly attired and beautifully decorated with jewellery, which will attract the attention of men who look at her when they pass along the road. She should not, however, show herself off shamelessly, as this would have the immediate effect of diminishing her value by half. She must sit in a place where she can easily be seen by the passers-by but she should not display her breasts. A courtesan's value is rather like that of the products on sale in the bazaar. She must engage a pimp who knows how to recruit clients and who will break their attachment to the other girls, as well as protecting her and acting as her bodyguard. There are many people who can do this kind of occupation, including guards or policemen, lawyers, astrologers, learned men, administrators, flower sellers and beggars. She should only sleep with a man if he is rich and independent. Suitable men whom she may take up with include those who are free from any ties, those who have influence with the King or his ministers and an only son whose father is wealthy, as well as those who have other excellent qualities and can therefore be resorted to for the sake of love and fame.

A courtesan, well dressed and wearing her ornaments, should sit or stand at the door of her house, and without exposing herself too much, should look on the public road so as to be seen by the passers-by, she being like an object on view for sale.

Kama Sutra

Expert in love

A courtesan should be pretty, young, gentle and skilled in the
art of pleasant conversation. She should be ready for sexual
relations and appreciate a man's qualities, not only in terms
of money but also of love. She should be expert in love and
always make love lovingly, with a preference for long-term
love affairs. She should know what she wants and behave
according to her inclinations. She should be eager to acquire
new knowledge, generous and keen on parties. There are
certain men who are not fit for relations with courtesans and
whom she should avoid, including those who are ill or
consumptive, those with worms in their stomach or bad
breath, and those who are in love with their wives, as well as
brutal men who are in the habit of hitting their wives or
servants. A courtesan should never sacrifice money for love,
and money should always be preferred to love. A woman
should take into account a man's importance before deciding
whether or not to sleep with him and, when she is
propositioned, she should never accept his advances at once.
Men have no respect for easy women and what is too easy
has no value.

*When a courtesan consorts with men she should cause each of
them to give her money as well as pleasure. . .*

Kama Sutra

A sign of affection

The courtesan's secretary should bring the man to her house
on the pretext of watching fights between quails, cocks or
rams, or to listen to mynah birds or parrots talk, or to attend
some artistic show. When the man comes to her dwelling, the
courtesan should give him some sign of her affection, such as
a present that will produce pleasure, curiosity and love in his
heart. After they have had an agreeable conversation, she
should then order a female servant to send him back home.
In order to find out what his intentions are, she should send
him a gift, but she should not allow him to come inside her
house. Her secretary should explain that she will shortly be
leaving for a trip and she should invite him to come back
later. When he returns to see her, he will bring her a mixture
of betel nuts and betel leaves, garlands of flowers and various
beauty products. As a mark of her affection for him, she
should also give him gifts in return, and indicate that she is
prepared to sleep with him and to have amorous relations
with him.

*. . . when the man comes to her house, the woman should give him
something capable of producing curiosity and love in his heart, such
as an affectionate present . . . She should also amuse him for a long
time by telling him such stories and doing such things as he may take
most delight in.*

Kama Sutra

Living the life of a wife

In order to please the man to whom she is attached, she should behave like a faithful wife and should strive to please him. A courtesan living the life of a wife is not troubled with too many lovers, while obtaining an abundance of wealth. She should charm him by pretending that she is in love with him and that this is the first time she has been attached to anyone, but she should not genuinely fall in love with him. The question of money should not, as yet, appear to be of any importance and she should tell him about her domineering mother (making one up if necessary), who is dependent on her and looks upon her daughter's money as her main interest in life. The courtesan should pretend to be suffering from an illness ~ nothing dangerous or contagious! ~ which will give her a pretext for going somewhere else to sleep with her other lovers. She teaches him the sixty-four arts, while pretending to be his pupil, and when they make love she makes out that she is quite ignorant of erotic techniques. He is therefore quite convinced that it is due to his efforts that she experiences pleasure.

When a courtesan is living as a wife with her lover, she should behave like a chaste woman, and do everything to his satisfaction. Her duty in this respect, in short, is that she should give him pleasure but should not become attached to him, though behaving as if she were really attached.

Kama Sutra

Extracting her livelihood

Once she is in control of her lover, the courtesan makes sure that she extracts her livelihood from him. She can do this in two ways: usually, the money is paid, quite simply, as the wages of love. But according to Vatsyayana, she can persuade him to give her double the normal price by using certain procedures. She might take money from him on the pretext of buying sweetmeats or other foods, clothes, flowers or perfumes and then either not buying them or claiming that they cost more than they actually did. Or she might flatter him and encourage him to show his generosity. She could claim that she needs to buy gifts for special religious festivals and ask him to contribute as proof of his affection. Or she could say that her jewels have been stolen when she was on the way to his house. Or perhaps she has been ruined because her house has burned down. Or she has engaged artists to do something for her lover. Or she has had to pay the expenses of the marriage ceremony of the son of a female friend. Or she has been ill and has to pay a lot of money for expensive treatment.

Money is got out of a lover in two ways: By natural or lawful means, and by artifices . . . Vatsyayana lays down that . . . when she makes use of artifice he gives her double money, and therefore artifice should be resorted to for the purpose of extorting money from him at all events.

Kama Sutra

Getting rid of her lover

When a courtesan decides that separation from her lover is inevitable ~ perhaps because she wants to take up with another lover, or she has noticed a change in his attitude to her, or he gives her too little money ~ there are several ways in which she can get rid of him. She can either be open about her intentions, or she can go about it discreetly. If she decides to do the latter, she can do things that she knows he doesn't like, or she can refuse to let him kiss her, or she can seek the company of other men, or she can refuse to sleep with him, or she can object to the wounds that he makes on her body with his nails and teeth, or she can pretend she is tired, or she can interrupt him in the middle of his stories, or she can refuse to see him. And she need not feel bad about this: in plying her trade, the courtesan earns her due; and in sleeping with her, the man should not have created a close bond, since she only did it for the money. So her conscience is clear.

When a courtesan intends to abandon a particular lover and take up with another one; or when she has reason to believe that her lover will shortly leave her, and return to his wives . . . she should, under any of these circumstances, endeavour to get as much money as she can from him as soon as possible.

Kama Sutra

tonics
and
potions

If nature has not been kind, a person should not be reluctant to use artificial aids to make them more beautiful in the eyes of others. Nor should they be frightened of resorting to the help of aphrodisiacs if their sexual relations are not satisfactory.

A person's beauty depends on many things, including the colour of their skin and hair, and their physical fitness. Some of these qualities are gratifyingly permanent whereas others will decline as a person grows old. An attractive appearance is probably the main and the most natural means of making a person agreeable in the eyes of others, but if someone's physical beauty leaves a lot to be desired, they should not hesitate to use any artificial means available to make them more attractive. Both the face and body can be painted, for instance, with special ointments and creams that have been made from the roots, leaves and flowers of various aromatic plants and which will immediately increase a person's sexual attraction. One example of this is the fine powder that can be made from plants such as the *Tabernaemontana coronaria,* the *Costus speciosus* or *arabicus,* and the *Flacourtia Cataphracta.* This powder should be applied to the wick of a lamp, which is then made to burn with the oil of blue vitriol, and the black pigment or lampblack that is produced should be applied to the eyelashes. This will have the immediate effect of making someone who does this look lovely.

If a fine powder is made of the above plants, and applied to the wick of a lamp, which is made to burn with the oil of blue vitriol, the black pigment or lampblack produced therefrom, when applied to the eyelashes, has the effect of making a person look lovely.

Kama Sutra

Increasing sexual attraction

There are several other interesting recipes for making special
ointments that are said to increase a person's sexual
attraction. The roots of several plants, including *Boerhavia
diffusa, Costus speciosus, Ethita pulescens, Hermidermus indicus*
and *Barleria prionitis*, for example, should be gathered together
with water lilies or blue lotus. These are then cooked and
made into a cream for massaging into the body, whereupon
it enhances both beauty and sexual attraction, and is also said
to bring good luck. At the same time, it is recommended that
the user also wear a necklace made of the flowers mentioned
and that this will immediately add to the attractiveness of the
body. Another recommendation concerns a concoction of
plants which, when eaten, is reputed to make one more
attractive. Crush the flowers of pink and blue lotus, mixed
with snake's saffron. Allow the mixture to dry and then eat it
diluted with honey and ghee. This sweetmeat also has an
immediately cleansing effect. It will not make someone
attractive straight away, but will improve their appearance in a
month's time.

*Crush the flowers of pink lotus and blue lotus, mixed with snake's
saffron. Let it dry. These ingredients, consumed together with honey
or ghee, make one attractive.*

Kama Sutra

Means of seduction

There are many magical techniques that can be used as a reliable means of seduction. Many examples of this are given here. If, for example, a man smears his penis with a mixture of datura seeds, black pepper, long pepper and honey, without the woman's knowledge, she will be bewitched by him and will submit to his wishes without hesitation. Or if he crushes together a mixture made up of a leaf that was brought by the wind, some sandalwood that was used to anoint a corpse and a little powdered peacock's bone and then smothers his penis with the resultant paste before making love to her, she will immediately be subject to his power. If a man chops a ball of milk hedge into small pieces and sprinkles it with red arsenic and powdered fragments of sulphur, then lets it dry seven times and mixes it with honey before anointing his penis with the mixture, the woman will be sure to swear her allegiance to him. And if he mixes these powdered ingredients with the dung of a special species of monkey with a coloured face and scatters this on the girl, she will feel no attraction for anyone else.

If a man cuts into small pieces the sprouts of the vajnasunhi plant, and dips them into a mixture of red arsenic and sulphur, and then dries them seven times, and applies this powder mixed with honey to his lingam, he can subjugate a woman to his will directly he has sexual union with her . . .

Kama Sutra

The science of aphrodisiacs

Even if a man succeeds in making a woman submit to him, this is of little use to him if he is then unable to consummate the relationship because he finds himself to be impotent. The science of aphrodisiacs is therefore described in order to help increase a man's virility, and many examples of mixtures are described that will help do just this. Garlic, for example, should be mixed with white pepper and liquorice, and the mixture should then be cooked in cow's milk. Once the mixture has cooled down sufficiently, add sugar and drink the resulting beverage, which will both strengthen a man's prowess and increase his flow of sperm. Another recommendation is to boil a ram's testicles in sweetened milk and then drink the liquid, which will again increase his virility. Similarly, a man can crush the roots of sweet potatoes in cow's milk, together with kauncha seeds, sugar, honey and ghee. He should then use this to make biscuits with wheat flour and when he has eaten a large quantity of these biscuits, his sperm will acquire such force that he will be able to sleep with thousands of women who will end up asking for his pity.

Crush vidari roots in cow's milk, together with svayamgupta seeds, sugar, honey, and ghee. Use it to make biscuits with wheat flour. He who eats them, as many as suits him, can enjoy an unlimited number of women, the ancient masters tell us.

Kama Sutra

Increasing sexual vigour

There are various aphrodisiac formulas, which can be used to cure both organic weaknesses and lack of excitation. Men should study these in the treatises of ayurveda, as well as in medical treatises, sacred books and other works. They can also be learned by consulting with clever scholars, men of experience, physicians and magicians who are familiar with magic words. It is important that no methods are attempted that are likely to cause either pain or injury, or which are harmful to bodily health, or which involve any animals being killed, or which are mixed with unclean substances. It is important, too, to use only procedures which are not only holy but which are also known to be healthy, and which have been recommended to you by people who already have experience in these matters, or by friends whom you know to wish you well.

The means of producing love and sexual vigour should be learned from the science of medicine, from the Vedas, from those who are learned in the arts of magic, and from confidential relatives. No means should be tried which are . . . likely to cause injury to the body, which involve the death of animals, or which bring us in contact with impure things.

Kama Sutra

Enlarging the penis

The size of the penis varies greatly from very small to huge, and a man who has a small penis can have recourse to various artificial aids. If a sensual and erotic man is keen to try to enlarge the size of his penis, he should learn how from an expert. One way is to rub the penis for ten nights with the hairs of a particular insect which lives in trees. Other creatures that live in trees are not suitable. Simply take hold of the insect with tweezers and rub it on the sides of the penis. The hairs will eventually fall out, as they are detached by the continual rubbing action, and they should then be spread out on the penis and massaged into the skin with oil. This will cause a swelling. When you think the penis is sufficiently swollen, lie on a bed and let the penis hang through a hole in the bed, which will make it get longer. When you have obtained the desired result, you can then remove the pain by using a cooking mixture, consisting of five astringents. The swelling brought on by this method is permanent and lasts for life.

When a man wishes to enlarge his lingam, he should rub it with the bristles of certain insects that live in trees, and then, after rubbing it for ten nights with oils, he should again rub it with the bristles as before. By continuing to do this a swelling will be gradually produced in the lingam . . .

Kama Sutra

Just as a penis can vary greatly in size, so too can a woman's vagina, which can be either large as in an elephant woman, or really tiny as in a deer woman. Something can be done about both these conditions if the woman is dissatisfied with them and they are causing her unhappiness, particularly if her dimensions are not compatible with those of her husband. An elephant woman, for example, who is concerned about the enormous size of her vulva, should crush the seeds of the white *Asteracantha longifolia* plant in water, and then smear her vulva with this paste. When it is treated in this way, even the biggest vulva will suddenly contract overnight and will become as narrow as that of a deer woman. Similarly, a deer woman who is worried that her vulva is overly small should make an ointment from the seeds of the pink lotus and the blue water lily in ghee and honey and apply this to her vulva. The ointment will widen her vulva miraculously to the dimensions of the elephant woman in just one single night.

An ointment made of the fruit of the Asteracantha longifolia (kokilaksha) will contract the yoni of a Hastini, or elephant woman, and this contraction lasts for one night. An ointment made by pounding the roots of the Nelumbium speciosum and of the blue lotus, and the powder of the plant Physalis flexuosa mixed with ghee and honey, will enlarge the yoni of the Mirigi, or deer woman.

Kama Sutra

Executive Editor *Jane McIntosh*

Editors *Katey Day and Nicola Hodgson*

Creative Director *Keith Martin*

Design Manager *Bryan Dunn*

Senior Designer *Claire Harvey*

Designers *Charlotte Barnes and Adrian Hutchins*

Picture Researcher *Wendy Gay*

Production Controller *Lucy Woodhead*

Front cover: BRIDGEMAN ART LIBRARY/PRIVATE COLLECTION, INDIA
Front cover background: E. T. ARCHIVE/VICTORIA & ALBERT MUSEUM,
LONDON
Back cover: E. T. ARCHIVE/VICTORIA & ALBERT MUSEUM, LONDON
Back flap bottom: BRIDGEMAN ART LIBRARY/PRIVATE COLLECTION

AKG LONDON/British Library, London 20/Chandigarh Museum 36/Jean-Louis
Nou 10, 68, 70, 94, 116, 144, 156, 166/National Museum of India, New Delhi 40.

BRIDGEMAN ART LIBRARY, LONDON/NEW YORK/Ashmolean Museum,
Oxford 140/British Library 12, 14, 16, 18, 44, 46, 58, 176/Fitzwilliam Museum,
University of Cambridge 30, 86, 88, 170/National Museum of India, New Delhi, India
48, 52, 64, 66, 72, 180/Private Collection 24, 32, 38, 54, 90, 92, 96, 110, 124, 138, 148,
160, 162, 168, 182, 184, 188/Victoria & Albert Museum, London 34, 60, 62, 98, 100,
106, 108, 112, 122, 142, 150, 158/Victor Lownes Collection, London 78.

CHRISTIE'S IMAGES, 8, 28, 50, 76, 132, 152, 154, 172, 178.

CORBIS-BETTMANN/Philadelphia Museum of Art 136.

E. T. ARCHIVE/British Library, Endpapers, 7, 9, 11, 13, 22, 33, 35, 37, 39, 41, 43, 45,
47, 49, 51, 53, 55, 56, 57, 59, 61, 130, 143, 145, 147, 149, 151, 153, 155, 157, 164/E.T.
Archive 80, 82, 84, 97, 99, 101, 102, 103, 104, 105, 107, 109, 113, 115, 117, 119, 121,
123, 125, 126, 128, 186/Marco Polo Gallery, Paris 6, 26/Marjorie Shoosmith 1-2, 95,
111/Victoria & Albert Museum, London 3- 4, 15, 17, 19, 21, 23, 25, 27, 29, 31, 63, 65,
67, 69, 71, 73, 74, 75, 77, 79, 81, 83, 85, 87, 89, 91, 93, 127, 129, 131, 133, 134, 135,
137, 139, 141, 146, 159, 161, 163, 165, 167, 169, 171, 173, 174, 175, 177, 179, 181, 183,
185, 187, 189.

WERNER FORMAN ARCHIVE/Private Collection 5, 42, 114/Philip Goldman
Collection 118, 120.